Construction Handbook for Minecraft

Collector's Edition

Table of Contents

Construction Handbook: The Collector's Edition

You now possess the most insightful, powerful, and inspirational guide to Buildings and Construction ever created! This guide will feature some of the most sought-after and game-changing designs the world has ever seen!

This special Collector's Edition features exciting new content that is sure to blow you away! The carefully selected articles presented will change the way you think about Minecraft forever!

Introduction

Minecraft is one of the most popular video games in the world, and one of the main reasons for this is the ability for just about anyone to jump into the game, and build anything they can dream of. There really is no limit to what you can create, only your imagination is holding you back!

But that doesn't mean that it's not a good idea to get some helpful tips from others along the way. Minecraft has been around for a long time now, and there are some very experienced builders out there. So in this guide, we hope we can provide you with the basic skills and ideas you can use to create something amazing and original in the world of Minecraftia!

Citadel of Beauty

This breathtaking design really shows off how important arches and other circular designs can be. This amazing build stands tall against a chilled backdrop of cool peaks.

The Battlestar Galactica by Ragnur Le Barbare

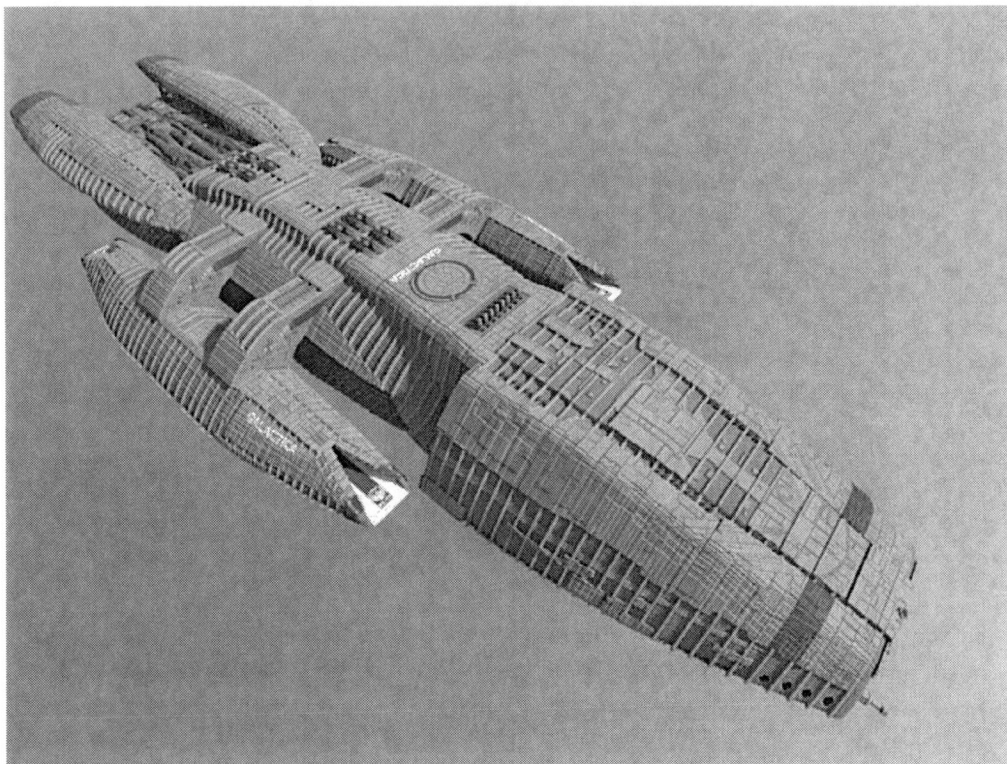

Up next is one of my favorite creations. This user has tirelessly recreated the entirety of the starship The Battlestar Galactica, from hand. It is not just an external model either, it is fully detailed inside too! Apparently it contains well over five MILLION blocks at this point, and he is still refining the build! Absolutely incredible!

Stark Tower

This incredibly accurate model of the Stark Tower featured in the Iron Man series really shows off how details can be the make or break aspect of any build! This tower is a striking representation of the wealth of Tony Stark!

The Apocalypse

Like any other aspect of an amazing build, ambience plays a key point in how a world is received by the viewer. This startling representation of a run-down city conveys a very unsettling tone!

The Winter Palace by Rigolo

Here we have what is regarded by many as one of the most detailed city building attempts to date. Youtuber "Rigolo" has worked with many others to create this amazingly detailed city.

Minas Tirith (From The Lord of the Rings) by Cornbass

Here we have one of the most impressive projects that I have come across. The whole city of Minas Tirith from The Lord of the Rings films, made entirely in Minecraft! I can't even begin to imagine the amount of time and effort required to create something like this, and if this doesn't get your imagination going, I don't know what will!

Emerald Farming

Emerald Farming is a great way to obtain valuable items. Trading with Villagers to obtain emeralds is known as Emerald Farming. Here is an example of an Emerald Farm.

Storage Rooms

For people with lots of items, a larger storage room is needed. Using Trapped Chests, a wall of chests can be created. Add an item frame with an item that represents what each chest contains to complete to room!

Sandstone Mansion

Smooth Sandstone is a great material to use in building mansions. It goes great with diamonds and quartz, as well as stone brick.

Pyramids

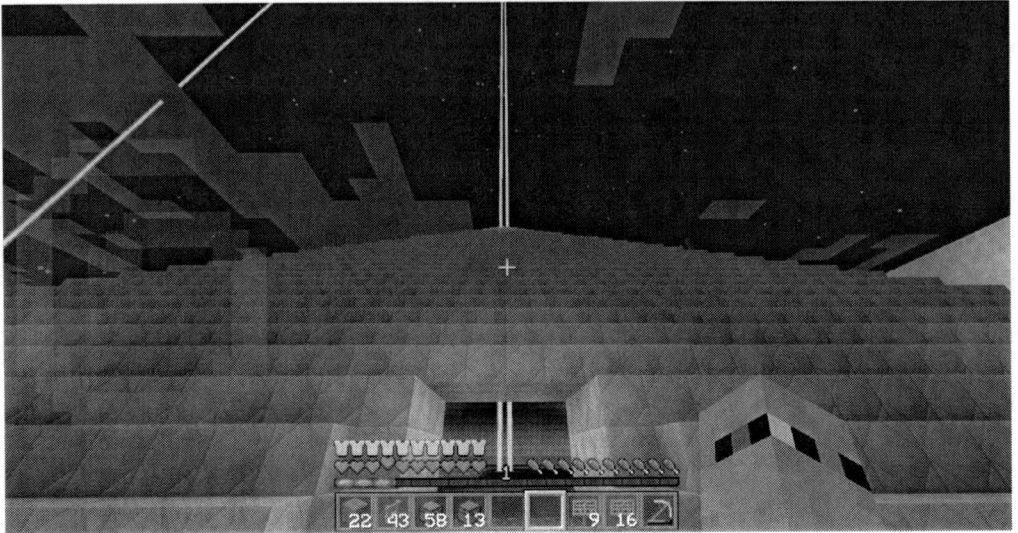

Pyramids are fun to build because of their simplistic design and versatility. Pyramids can be made out of any block! Decorate the inside however you like. You could create a maze, storage room, house, or whatever else you could think of!

Water Features

Add some flare to your build by adding Water Features! A fountain, pool, or even a bathtub are all great ways to incorporate water into your design.

Ancient Ruins

Deep in the jungle you find yourself a ruined temple! Use lots of cracked and mossy stone to build this haunting creation

Jail

That Villager is up to no good! Throw him in the slammer!

Tanks

Got creeper problems? Blow them away
with your very own fleet of heavy duty tanks!

Pirate Ship

Sail off into the land of blocks and creepers in an amazing Pirate Ship. Use wool for the masts, and create an awesome poop-deck!

Military Barracks

Now your army of villagers will have a comfortable place to rest before battling hordes of creepers.

Yacht

Live a life of luxury in a super-large yacht!

Spaceships

In Minecraft, spaceships can be very complex!

Pixel Art

Using coloured wool, Pixel Art can be created! Almost anything can be created with pixel art, from video game characters to flowers to cars!

Helicopter

Escape the wrath of the Wither in a Helicopter!

Graveyard

Visit the souls of those lost in Minecraft. Build a memorial to your fallen friends!

Hotels

Need a place to sleep? No problem! Charge your friends a diamond every time they sleep in this beautiful hotel

Robots

Gigantic robots are always a welcomed sight!

3D Models

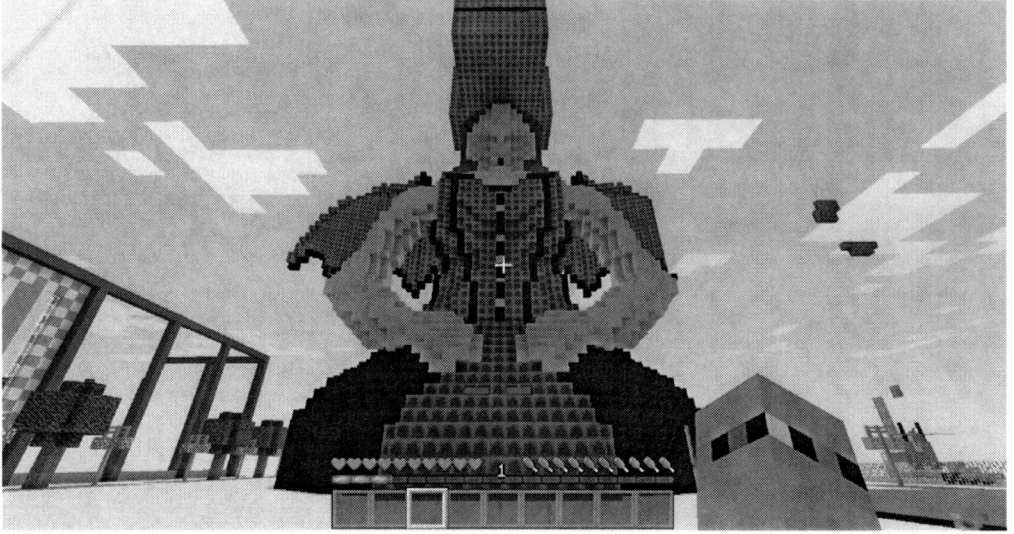

Have somebody you want to build? It can be done!

Museum

Have something you want to show off? Did you finally get a Wither Skull? Put it in a museum! Use item frames to hold items!

Town Hall

Perfect place for all the villagers to discuss what they are going to be trading next!

Navy Destroyer

A large Navy Vessel in Minecraft is always a great build!

Death Star

It might be broken, but it's definitely not forgotten!

Bridge

Cross that pool of lava in style!

Cities

Build up your very own metropolis!

Volcano

Watch out for that lava!

Barn

Make a nice home for your animals!

Harbour

A safe place to unload all the precious cargo from your mining adventures!

Theme Park

Even Villagers need to have some fun once in a while

Mountains

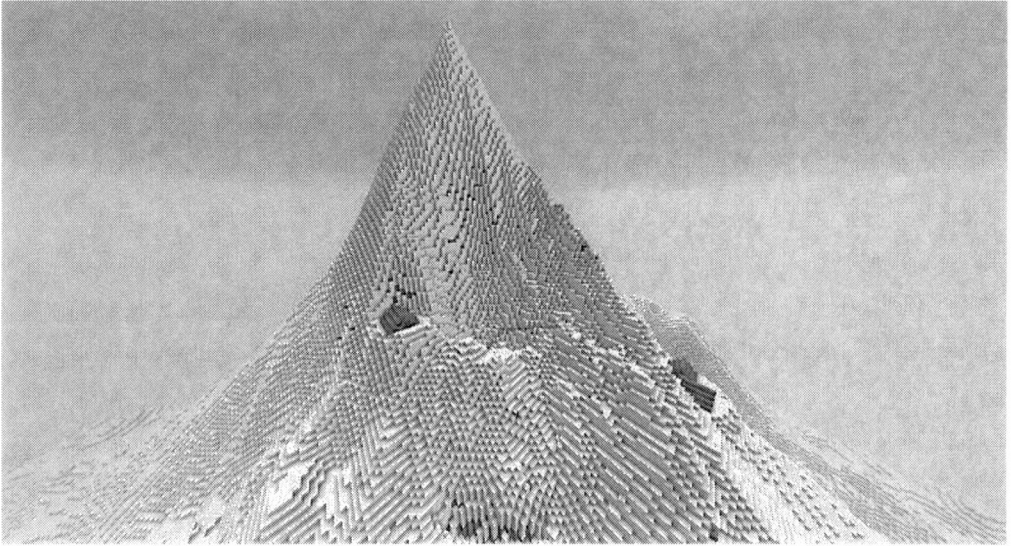

Scale the icy slope and make it to the peak of the gigantic mountain!

Ski Resort

If climbing mountains isn't your cup of tea, then you should relax at a ski lodge!

Hockey Arena

Challenge your friends to an ice-cold game of hockey!

Basketball Court

Can that Villager even dunk?

Colosseum

Travel back in time and fight gladiators!

The Globe Theatre

If gladiators scare you, perhaps watching a Shakespearean play would be more appealing!

Eiffel Tower

Take a trip to Paris without leaving your living room!

McDonald's

Hungry? Why not build your very own fast food joint?!

Bank

Need to make a deposit? Make sure the creeper doesn't blow up the vault!

Submarine

Do some deep-sea diving in this amazing vessel!

Small Race Car

Step 1:

Make a 7x3 frame with Black Wool

Step 2:

Fill in with stone slabs

Step 3:

Place stone slabs on top

Step 4:

Saved screenshot as 2014-06-28_16.31.02.png

Raise the back stone slab up to 3

Step 5:

Using 3 stone slabs, make a spoiler

Step 6:

Dig one block down and replace it with a stone slab. Put a rail on top of that.

Step 7:

Add a minecart and hop in!

2x2 Redstone Door

Step 1:

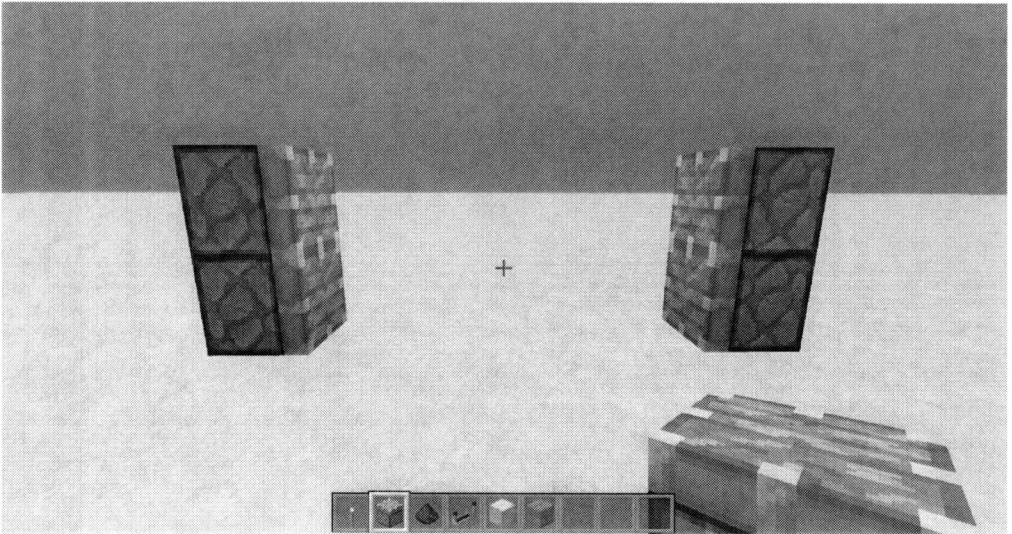

Place sticky pistons 6 blocks apart

Step 2:

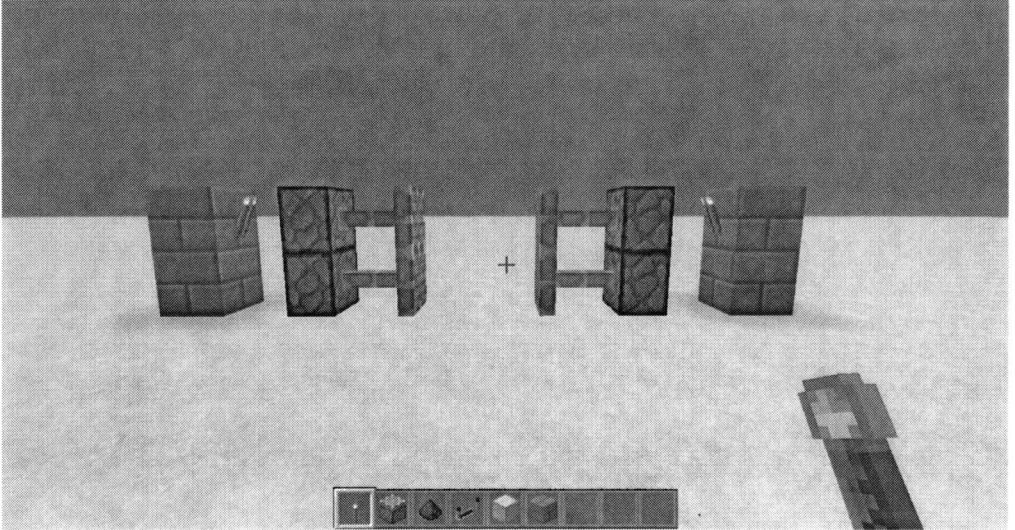

Make a 2 tall tower 1 block behind the sticky pistons, and place a redstone torch on the side. This will activate the pistons

Step 3:

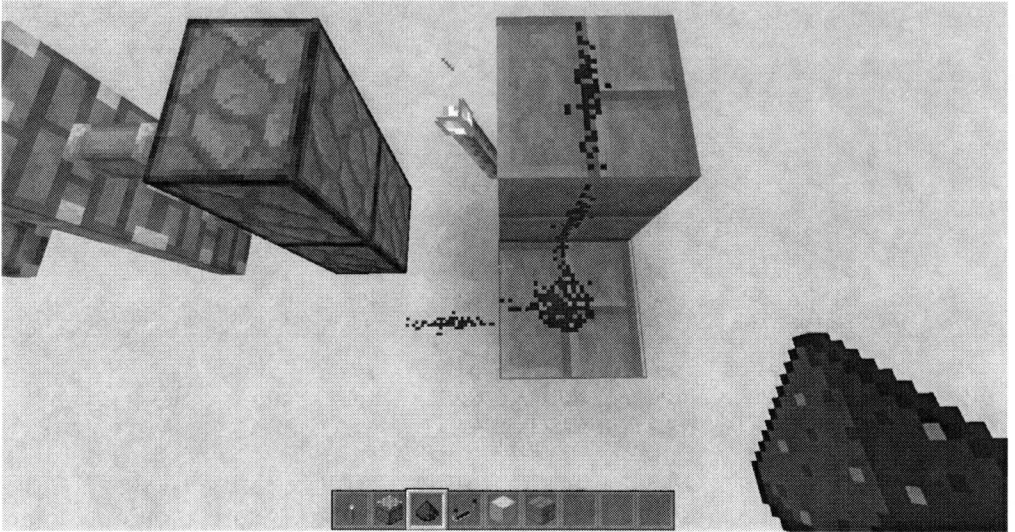

Make a redstone wire down…

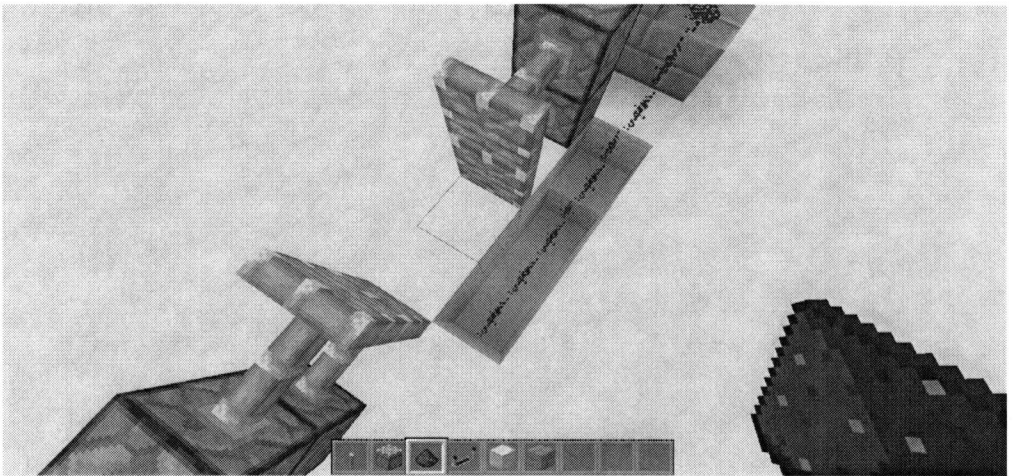

Into the ground, on both sides

Step 4:

Make a 2x3 redstone rectangle underneath the surface

Step 5:

Saved screenshot as 2014-06-28_16.45.47.png

Cover it up

Step 6:

Saved screenshot as 2014-06-28_16.45.56.png

Place pressure plates on the 2 blocks before and after the pistons

Step 7:

Place the blocks that will be the "door"

Step 8:

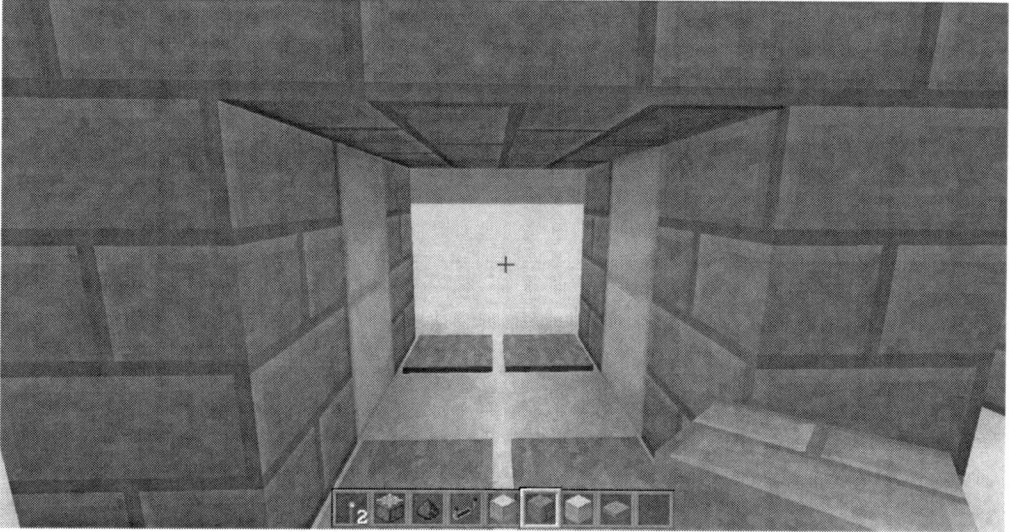

Seal and enjoy!

Water Elevator

Step 1:

Create a tower like this, any height

Step 2:

Saved screenshot as 2014-06-28_16.47.45.png

Create a 2-tall opening at the bottom

Step 3:

Place signs every other block, starting from the 2nd block

Step 4:

Saved screenshot as 2014-06-28_16.49.04.png

Repeat Step 3 with water, placing it between the signs

Step 5:

Now walk into the bottom and hold {SPACE} to move up! Enjoy!

Obsidian Generator:

Step 1:

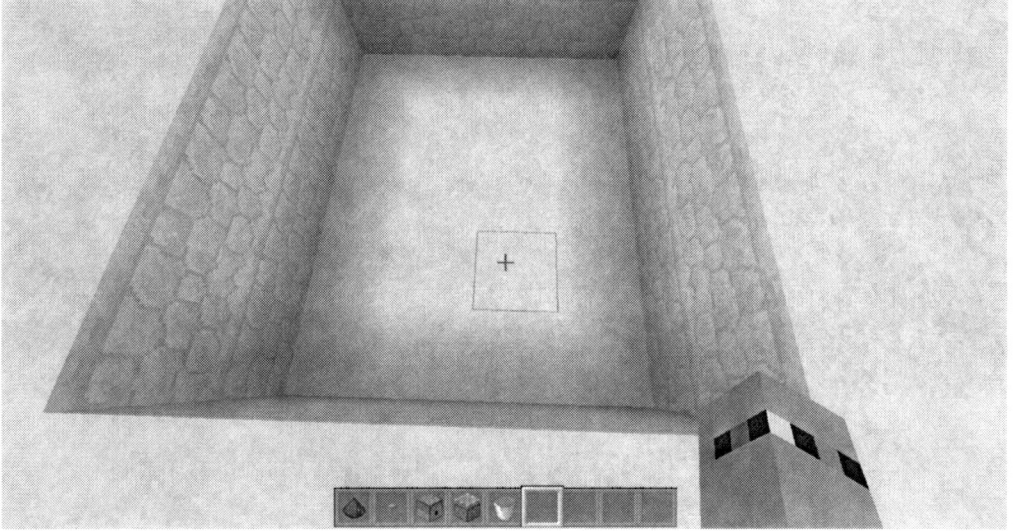

Dig a 5x4 hole, 2 blocks down

Step 2:

Dig one more block down on the sides

Step 3:

Saved screenshot as 2014-06-28_16.57.43.png

Dig 1 block into the wall

Step 4:

Add water to each block in this "shelf"

Step 5:

Place redstone

Step 6:

Using redstone, repeaters, pistons and dispensers, arrange the outside like this:

Step 7:

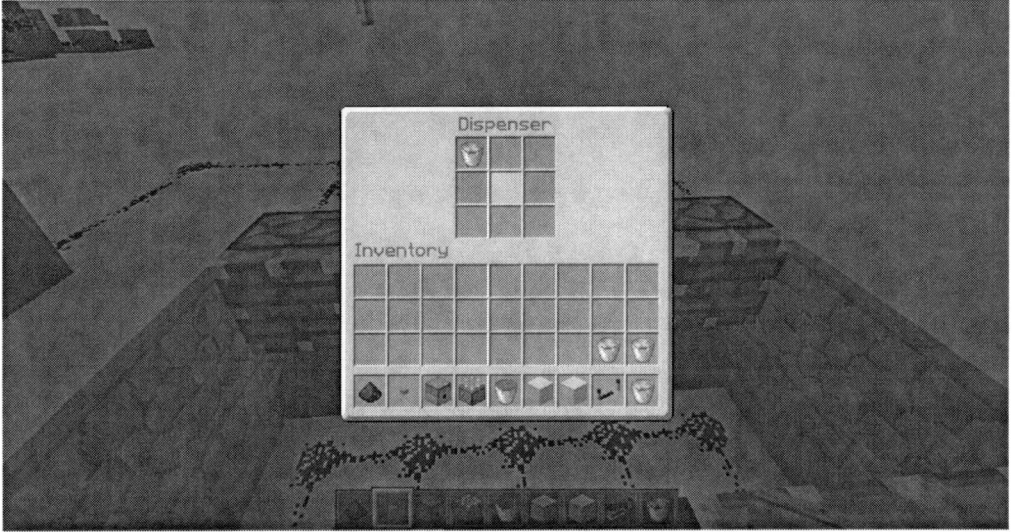

Put lava into the dispensers

Step 8:

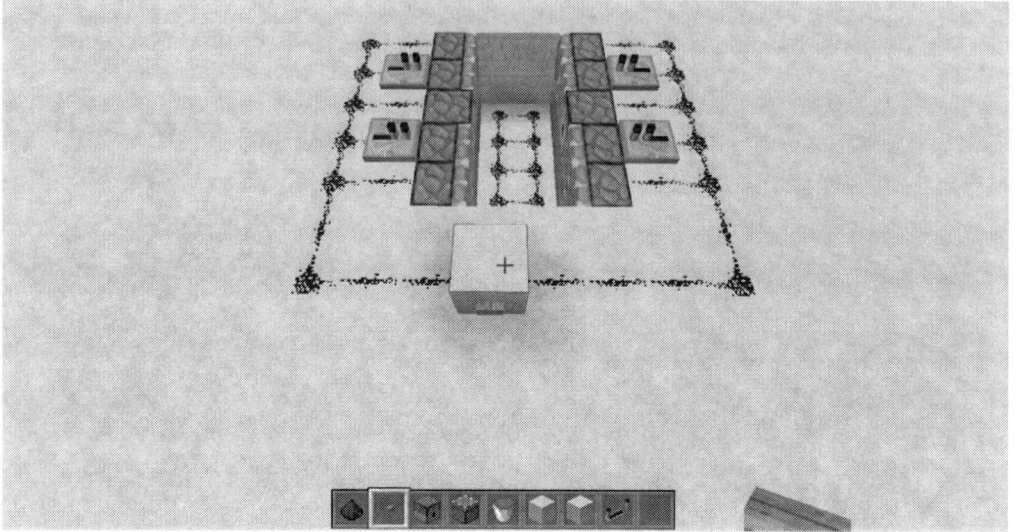

Connect the redstone circuit and add a button

Step 9:

Press the button and wait for the lava to cover all the redstone, then press it again. You will see that there is a nice sheet of obsidian to mine!

Jail:

Step 1:

Create a square or rectangle of stone brick. This can be any size.

Step 2:

Add stairs wherever you like

Step 3:

Make a doorway, and put up walls around the floor

Step 4:

Add furnishings for the prisoner, and make 2 windows out of iron fence

Step 5:

Add the jail cell bars using iron fence

Step 6:

Make a roof

Step 7:

Add Iron Doors, for extra protection

Step 8:

Enjoy your life with this prisoner locked up!

Redstone Flip Switch
This small contraption will allow buttons and pressure plates to work like levers

Step 1:

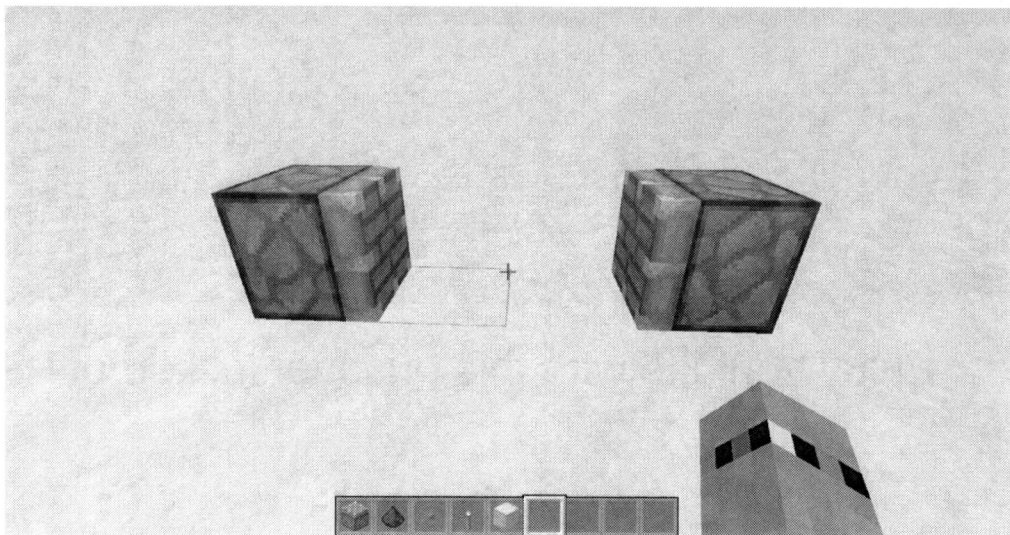

Place 2 sticky pistons 4 blocks apart

Step 2:

In front of one of the pistons, dig 1 block down and place a redstone torch

Step 3:

Place a block on top of the torch, and then 2 blocks above

Step 4:

Put redstone torches on each end, above the pistons

Step 5:

Place redstone on the 2 blocks, then bring it 1 block down. Add a button

Step 6:

This can now be used to power whatever redstone device you need, just make a redstone circuit off the end

Auto-Smelting

As of the 1.6 update, furnaces can now automatically smelt, by using hoppers and trapped chests to move items around

Step 1:

Place a chest, The hopper attached (hold shift and right click the chest while holding the hopper to attach). Place a furnace above the hopper

Step 2:

Attach a hopper to the side of the furnace, and another one above

Step 3:

Place a chest above one of the hoppers, and a trapped chest above the other. Label the chest directly above the furnace as "Material" and the other as "Fuel"

Step 4:

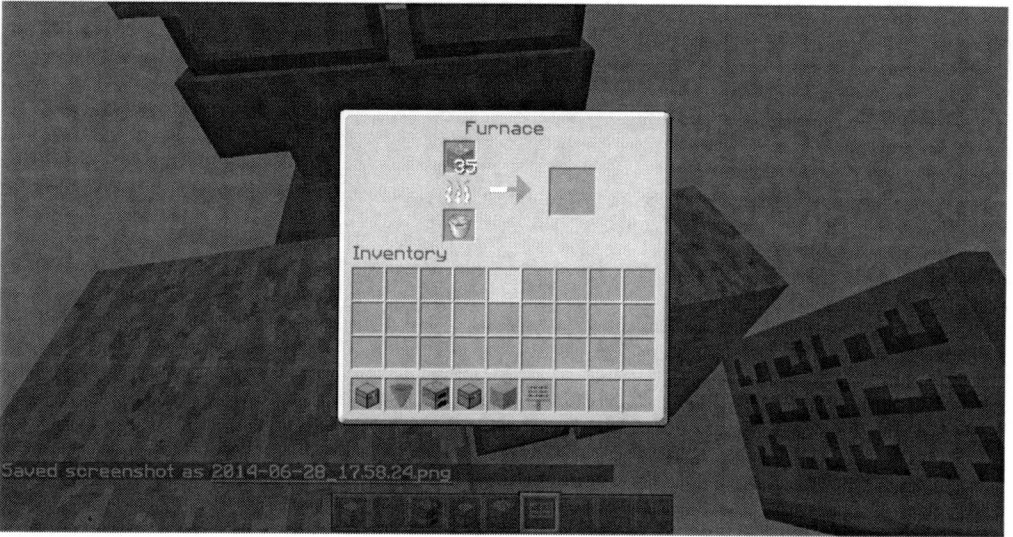

Now when you place your items in the respective chest, the furnace will automatically start to smelt

Step 5:

The products will be found in the chest on the ground!

Sphere

Spheres are very complex shapes that can be made in Minecraft. It takes some time, but hard work always pays off.

Step 1:

Create a 1x7 tower 1 block off the ground

Step 2:

From the middle block, extend 3 blocks outward in all directions

Step 3:

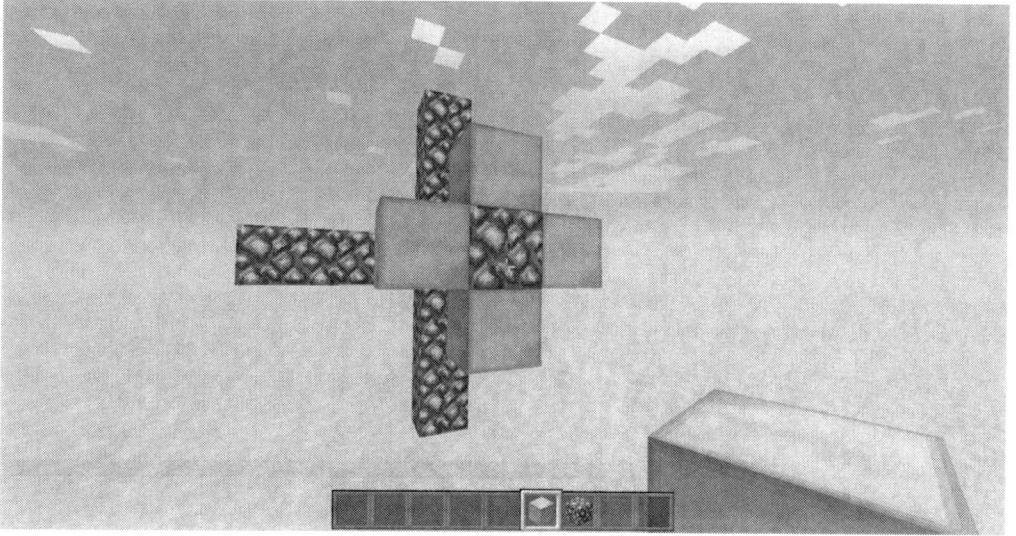

At the end of each shaft, put your block of choice around the edges.

Step 4:

Do this for each shaft

Step 5:

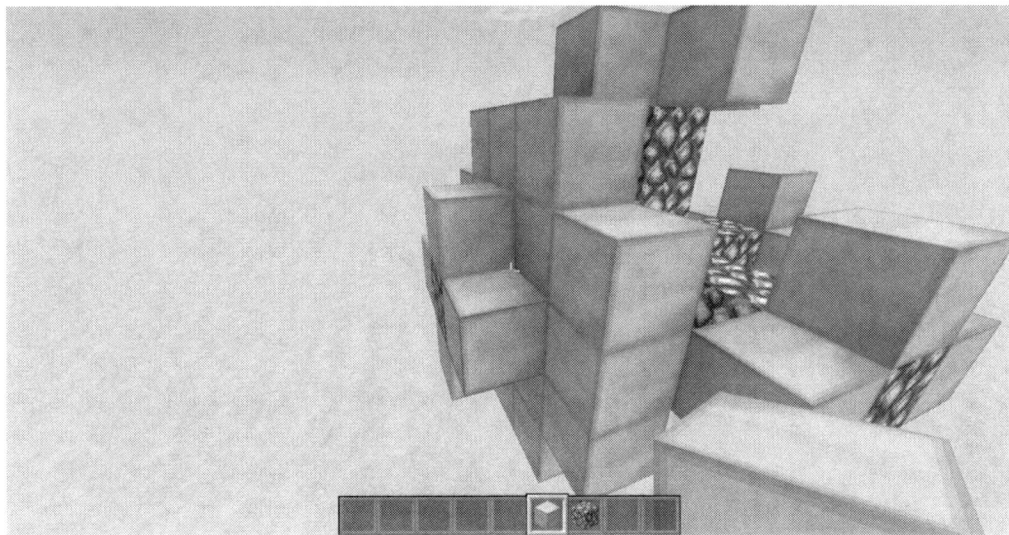

For the 4 shafts coming out from the middle, follow this pattern. Basically, make a square behind the end of the shaft and break off the corners.

Step 6:

When all middle shafts have been completed, you should be left with 4 holes on the top. Fill them in.

Step 6:

Do the same for the bottom, and you will have a perfect sphere!

Truck

Step 1

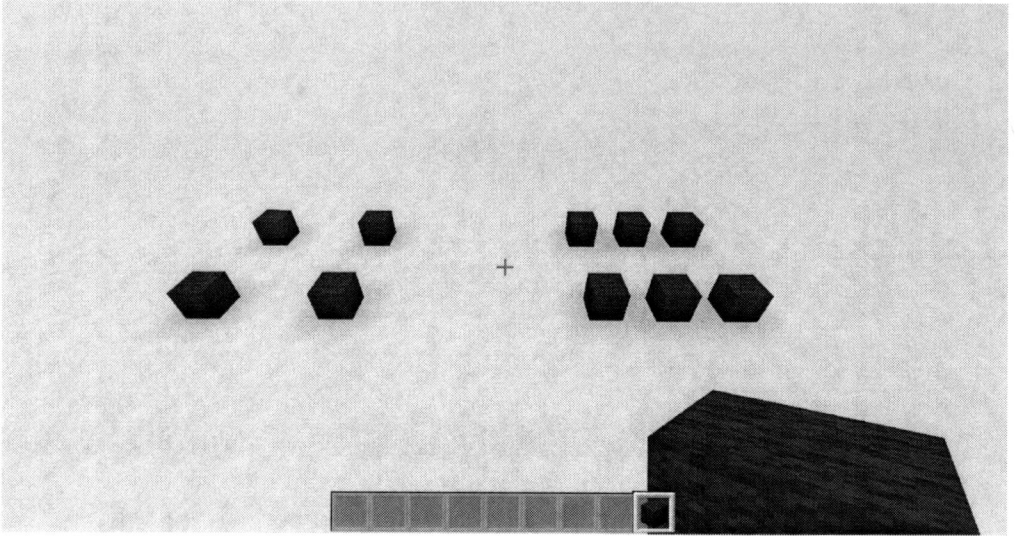

Place black wool in the following pattern. It can be adjusted to fit the size you want.

Step 2

Fill the front in with stone slabs

Step 3:

Construct the cabin

Step 4:

Fill in the trailer with stone slabs

Step 5:

Create the hitch between trailer and cabin

Step 6:

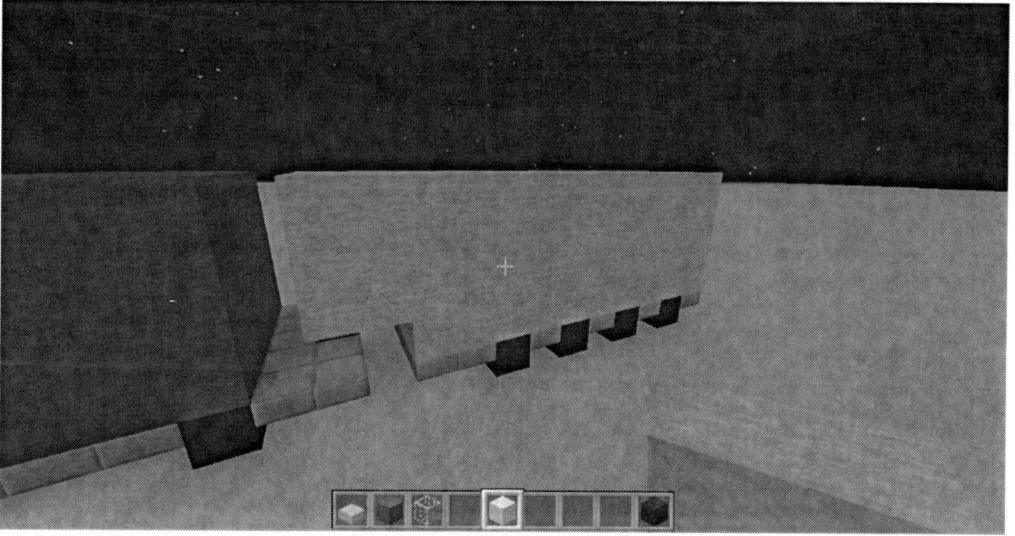

Build up the trailer.

Step 7:

Add the exhaust. Cobwebs can be used to look like smoke!

Step 8:

Add some details and you are good to go!

Conclusion

This guide has provided you with some insight and inspiration to begin your Minecraft projects. These examples should help server as an example of what can be accomplished with a little imagination, and a lot of heart.

CPSIA information can be obtained at www.ICGtesting.com
Printed in the USA
LVOW10s0307161214

419035LV00036B/1185/P